From Your Friends at **The MAILBOX®**

W9-BRN-771

Quick & Easy
SCIENCE FUN

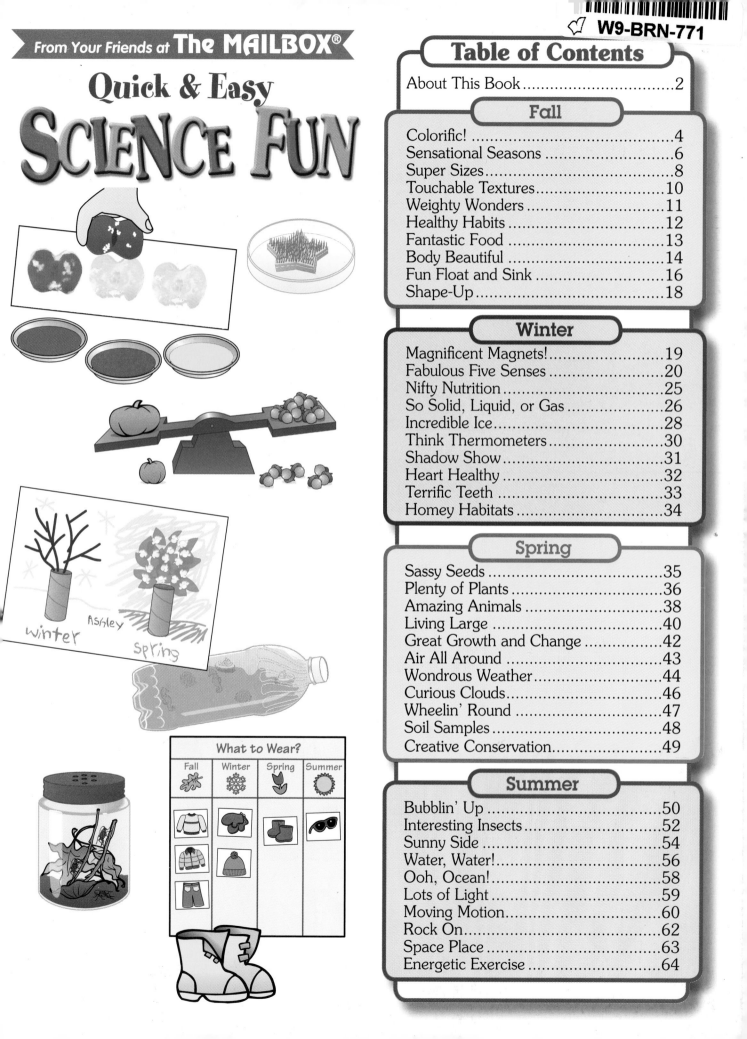

What to Wear?

Fall	Winter	Spring	Summer

Ashley
winter
spring

Table of Contents

About This Book

Designed to add zest to your science curriculum, *Quick & Easy Science Fun* is a wonderful collection of over 100 simple seasonal science experiments, activities, and demonstrations. Students will explore the wonders of science, develop science skills, and learn about a wealth of earth, life, and physical science topics through fun individual, small-group, and whole-class activities. These activities are perfect for supplementing your existing science curriculum. The pick-and-choose nature of the book allows you to quickly find just the right experiment, activity, or demonstration to complement your science curriculum. Although quick, simple, and fun, *Quick & Easy Science Fun* activities provide students with meaningful science experiences that support the National Science Education Standards.

Quick & Easy Science Fun

Managing Editor: Cindy K. Daoust

Editor at Large: Diane Badden

Staff Editors: Angie Kutzer, Jan Trautman

Writers: Beth Allison, Pamela Buescher, Kimberli Carrier, Lucia Kemp Henry, Angie Kutzer, Barbara Spillman Lawson, Kimberly Love, Suzanne Moore

Copy Editors: Karen Brewer Grossman, Amy Kirtley-Hill, Karen L. Mayworth, Debbie Shoffner

Cover Artists: Nick Greenwood, Clevell Harris

Art Coordinator: Rebecca Saunders

Artists: Pam Crane, Theresa Lewis Goode, Nick Greenwood, Clevell Harris, Ivy L. Koonce, Sheila Krill, Clint Moore, Greg D. Rieves, Rebecca Saunders, Barry Slate, Donna K. Teal

Typesetters: Lynette Dickerson, Mark Rainey

President, The Mailbox Book Company™: Joseph C. Bucci

Director of Book Planning and Development: Chris Poindexter

Book Development Managers: Cayce Guiliano, Elizabeth H. Lindsay, Thad McLaurin, Susan Walker

Curriculum Director: Karen P. Shelton

Traffic Manager: Lisa K. Pitts

Librarian: Dorothy C. McKinney

Editorial and Freelance Management: Karen A. Brudnak

Editorial Training: Irving P. Crump

Editorial Assistants: Hope Rodgers, Jan E. Witcher

Colorific!

(Physical Science)

Twisted Apple Prints

Youngsters will enjoy twisting up secondary color identification skills using this favorite fall fruit! To prepare, cut six apples in half and cut a supply of 4" x 12" white construction paper strips. Pour red, yellow, and blue tempera paint into three separate containers and gather a supply of paper towels. Invite a small group of youngsters to the center and explain that these *primary* colors (red, yellow, and blue) can be mixed together to create different colors. Invite a child to dip the flat side of an apple half into the yellow paint and then press it onto his strip of paper. Have him dip a different apple half into the blue paint, press it *on top* of the yellow print, and twist the apple slightly to mix the two colors together. Invite him to experiment mixing other color combinations in the same manner. (To reuse apples for printing, rinse with water and wipe dry with a paper towel.) To extend this activity, challenge each student to recreate two of his color combinations to make a color pattern on a clean strip of paper. Use the pattern strips as a border display on the "Autumn Rainbows" bulletin board below.

Yellow and blue make green!

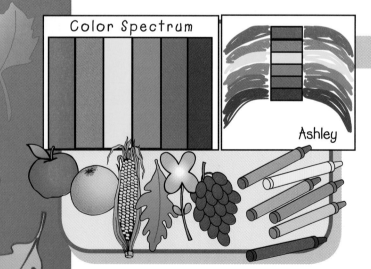

Color Spectrum

Ashley

Autumn's Rainbow

All the colors of a rainbow! Youngsters will learn about the *visible spectrum* with this color-matching art activity. In advance, gather an illustration of the spectrum or use wide strips of colored paper to create a chart as shown. Cut a class supply of 3" x 1" construction paper strips in each color and gather a variety of items in each color: red, orange, yellow, green, blue, purple. Ask youngsters to name each color on the spectrum and explain that the colors always appear in this order. Invite one student at a time to choose an item and place it in a row in front of the matching color on the spectrum chart. Repeat until each child has had a turn. Then give each child one strip of each rainbow color and ask her to glue them in order onto a sheet of white paper. (You may want to have a finished example for youngsters to use as a guide.) Then have her use crayons to complete her rainbow illustration as shown. Display the creations on a bulletin board titled "Autumn Rainbows."

Color Detectives

Take youngsters on a fun fall walk to search for seasonal colors and practice observation skills at the same time. In advance collect a class supply of fall-colored paint strip samples from a local paint store (duplicate color strips for several children will work). Also gather several fall items that match the color of your paint samples (acorns, pinecones, grass, flowers, colored leaves). Show youngsters the paint samples and the gathered items and compare the colors. Then give each child one color strip and ask him to look for matching color items during the walk. Upon returning, invite each child to show his color strip, name the color, and recall the matching items he observed. Discuss with youngsters the colors they see the most during the fall season. Save the leaves collected to use with "Colorful Change" below.

Colorful Change

Fall is a great season to show youngsters how things change over time, and colorful fall leaves provide a sensory experience. To prepare, collect a supply of unwrapped crayon pieces and white copy paper. Provide a variety of different-colored leaves for a small group of children to observe with a magnifying glass. Choose two leaves (one green and one with changing colors) to examine with youngsters. Discuss the differences in how each leaf looks, feels, and smells. Have each child choose one leaf and ask her to identify the colors and then find matching crayons. Ask her to use the selected crayons to create a colorful leaf rubbing. If desired, cut out each child's leaf rubbing and display it on a bulletin board.

Sensational Seasons

(Earth Science)

Signs of the Seasons

Investigate the signs of each season as youngsters practice classification skills. In advance, gather magazines and picture calendars and then cut four seasonal shapes from poster board as shown. If desired, take youngsters outside to observe the seasonal changes. Then divide youngsters into four groups and assign each group a different season (fall, winter, spring, summer). Help each group choose the shape that matches its assigned season. Ask each group to cut out magazine and calendar pictures that illustrate its season. Encourage each group to share pictures that belong to another group's season. Have each group glue its pictures onto the seasonal shape. Invite each group to present its creation to the class, and help the children explain why each picture represents the season. Display these seasonal signs in your classroom.

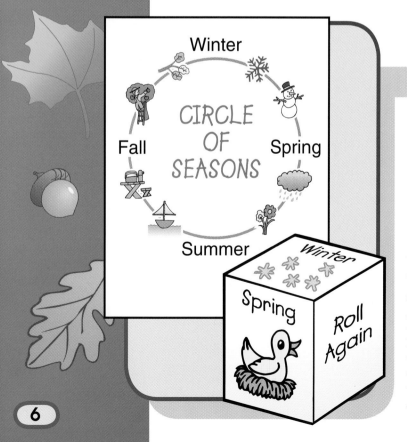

Circle of Seasons

Develop youngsters' communication skills as they describe and illustrate seasonal events with this small-group game. In advance, make a game cube by placing a seasonal picture on each side of a square tissue box and labeling as shown. Then draw a large circle on the board and label it as shown. To begin, ask a child to roll the cube, name the season, and then describe one activity that occurs during that season (swimming during summer, sledding during winter). Ask him to draw the event on the corresponding section of the circle after he passes the cube to the next player. Challenge youngsters to name the season that occurs before or after the one illustrated on the cube. Continue until each child has had a turn. Round and round the seasons go!

Scents of the Season

The nose knows! Youngsters will enjoy giving sensory descriptions of each season as they create a sweet-smelling chart. To prepare, collect a variety of dry spices (pumpkin pie spice, cinnamon), powdered drink mixes (hot chocolate, fruit drinks), powdered gelatin, and floral-scented talc. Place a small amount of each sample in a separate paper cup. Introduce the collection to youngsters and then invite each child to carefully smell each scent. Help youngsters classify scents that represent each season (pumpkin pie spice in fall, hot chocolate in winter) as you separate the scents into four groups. Give each child a sheet of construction paper divided into four sections and labeled as shown. Ask her to choose one scent for each season. Have her place a small amount of glue on each section of her chart and then sprinkle on a sample scent to represent each season. Have her draw a picture in each section to illustrate the seasonal scent. Invite each child to share her "scent-sational" chart, and help her describe why each scent reminds her of a particular season.

Seasonal Feeling

Get a feel for each season as youngsters use their senses to identify seasonal objects. In advance, collect a class supply of objects that are associated with each season (mittens, unbrellas, acorns, sunglasses, etc.). Place the objects in a bag. Label each season on a separate section of a sheet of chart paper. Blindfold one student and have him pull one object out of the bag. Ask him to describe the object using his sense of touch and smell. Challenge him to name to which season the object belongs. Remove the blindfold and ask him to place the object on the correct section of the chart as shown. Repeat until each child has had a turn. What a great feeling!

Super Sizes
(Physical Science)

Nutty Comparison

Compare size attributes and improve communication skills as youngsters complete this nutty activity. Prepare two charts as shown and collect a class supply of unshelled walnuts. (If any child is allergic to nuts, use plastic counters.) Place the chart on a table or on the floor. Give each child one walnut. Then invite one small group at a time to search the classroom to find two objects; one that is larger and one that is smaller than the walnut. Ask each group to place each object on the corresponding chart. Invite each child to choose one object from each chart and complete the following sentence orally for the group: A [block] is larger than the walnut and a [bead] is smaller than the walnut. If desired, write each sentence on a sheet of paper and give each child a page to illustrate. Then compile the pages into a class book.

What's smaller than the 🥜?

What's larger than the 🥜?

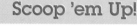

Alex

Scoop 'em Up!

How many scoops of birdseed fill a cup? Your little tweeties will flock to investigate with this tactile measurement activity. Gather three different-size plastic measuring cups (small, medium, large) and several plastic spoons. Partially fill a plastic tub with birdseed. To prepare, ask each child to draw and color a small, a medium, and a large cup on his paper as shown. Invite a child to count the number of spoonfuls required to fill the small cup with birdseed. Have each child record the number on his sheet of paper. Then have two more children repeat the activity, one with the medium and one with the large cup. Ask youngsters to compare the number of scoops and the size of each cup. To vary the activity, replace the plastic spoons with three-ounce plastic cups and use in a center for further investigation.

Rollin' Around

Use this unique size comparison activity to introduce youngsters to measuring circumference. In advance, gather two thumbtacks, a small pumpkin, and an apple. Push one tack into the pumpkin and the other into the apple as shown. Stock a center with several lengths of bulletin board paper, crayons, and counting cubes. Invite a pair of youngsters to the center. Then model for the pair how to measure each fruit. First, color a large dot on the left side of a sheet of bulletin board paper. Next, place the pumpkin on the paper with the thumbtack beside the dot and touching the paper. Then slowly roll the pumpkin over until the thumbtack has touched the paper again; draw another dot to mark the ending location. Finally, place a line of cubes between the two dots and count them. If desired, write the number of cubes used on the paper. Measure the apple on the same sheet of paper using the same directions. Then compare the results. Ready, set, roll!

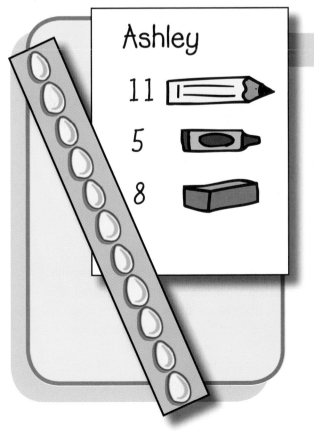

Ashley

11

5

8

Seed Sticks

Guide youngsters to create this fun nonstandard ruler to practice measurement skills. To prepare, cut a class supply of 6" x 2" poster board strips and collect dried pumpkin seeds. To make one ruler, glue seeds end to end on the strip and let it dry. Invite each child to use her seed ruler to measure lengths of various classroom objects by counting the number of seeds. Have her record her answers on a sheet of paper by illustrating a picture of each object and writing the number of seeds counted for each one. Challenge each child to find two objects that are the same length. Later have each child share her findings with the class.

Touchable Textures
(Physical Science)

Touch and Tell

Get that great fall feeling! Help youngsters practice their communication skills as they touch and describe physical attributes of seasonal objects. In advance, collect acorns, pinecones, leaves, apples, pumpkin seeds, and other fall-related objects. Place the collection inside a plastic pumpkin. Create a class texture graph as shown. Invite a child to place one hand inside the container, describe how one object feels (bumpy, smooth, etc.), and try to identify it. Have him pull the item out of the container to check. Ask him to draw the object on the graph and color the corresponding texture squares. Repeat the activity until all objects have been identified. If desired, place a different set of items in the plastic pumpkin and repeat the steps above. Then place this activity at a center for youngsters to investigate more.

I'm a Macintosh!

Tactile Apples

Treat youngsters' senses as they investigate this favorite fall snack. Gather several different types of apples and a container of applesauce. You will also need a class supply of paper cups and plastic spoons. Ask a small group of youngsters to feel each type of apple and describe the different textures. Encourage youngsters to compare the similarities and differences in shape, size, and texture of the apples. Then slice each apple and remove a few seeds from each one. Have youngsters compare the shape, size, and texture of the different apple seeds. Then give each child an apple slice and a spoonful of applesauce to compare the textures as they taste each one. "Apple-icious"!

Weighty Wonders

(Physical Science)

How Heavy?

Worth their weight in candy corn? Use this sweet activity to give youngsters practice comparing weight. In advance, partially fill four resealable plastic bags with varying amounts of candy corn. For durability, secure the edges of each bag with tape. Demonstrate for a small group of youngsters how to hold two bags to determine which is heavier. Encourage language skills by asking each child to describe and compare the bags as he holds them. Then ask the group to work together to place the bags in order from heaviest to lightest.

Nutty Predictions

Nutty Predictions			
Kastin	20	Paula	20
Alex	10	Jesse	55
Janet	5	Shandi	40
Larry	15	Ron	15
Seth	12	Sandy	25
Hope	8	Colby	30

Pumpkins, pumpkins! Help youngsters practice prediction skills as they ponder the weight of pumpkins. Gather a small pumpkin, an even smaller pumpkin, a supply of acorns or unshelled nuts, and a balance scale. (If any child is allergic to nuts, use plastic counters.) Prepare a chart as shown. Show youngsters the pumpkins and acorns. Place one pumpkin on the balance scale. Ask each child to predict how many acorns it will take to balance the weight of the pumpkin. Record youngsters' predictions on the chart. Have youngsters help place acorns on the scale to balance the pumpkin. Then help youngsters count the acorns and compare the result to their predictions. Repeat the process with the remaining pumpkin. Place this activity at a center for further practice.

Healthy Habits

(Life Science)

Aaah-choo!

Grab a tissue to help teach youngsters how germs can be spread with this sneezy demonstration. Fill a mist-type spray bottle with water and create a nose-shaped cutout to tape onto it as shown. First, spray water onto surfaces normally touched by youngsters (doorknob, water faucet, etc.) as you pretend to sneeze. Then ask a child to touch each surface and compare it to touching germs from a real sneeze. Next, spray a "sneeze" directed toward youngsters and discuss how this action spreads germs. Spray directly into a child's hand, and discuss how some of the germs were caught in his hand and no one else was sprayed this time. Then shake hands with the child and discuss how the germs were passed between your hands. Finally, spray a sneeze directly onto a tissue and then shake hands with a child. Discuss how the tissue helps catch the germs and keeps hands dry and germ free too.

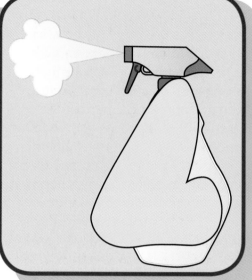

Handy Washing

Emphasize the importance of hand washing with this hands-on activity. To prepare, gather several slices of white bread and unsweetened cocoa powder. Discuss with youngsters why it is so important to wash hands often and especially before eating. Then dust a child's hands with a small amount of cocoa to represent dirty hands. Give her a slice of bread to knead for a few seconds as youngsters observe. Have her wash her hands and then give her another slice of bread to knead as youngsters observe. Compare the two pieces of bread. Discuss with youngsters how germs transfer from dirty hands to food eaten. How handy!

Fantastic Food
(Life Science)

Apple I.D.

Apples, apples, apples! Apple varieties are great for practicing classification and sorting skills. Choose three or four distinctively different apple types, gathering several of each type. Locate a picture of each type of apple by checking grocery store advertisements or seed catalogs (or draw your own illustrations). Glue each apple picture onto a card as shown. Mix all the apples together. Have youngsters work together to classify the apples, using the picture cards as a reference. Discuss the similarities and differences in the types of apples. Then offer youngsters a sample of each type of apple and discuss the similarities and differences in taste and texture. So many apples, so much learning!

Golden Delicious

Granny Smith

Red Delicious

Will all the popcorn pop?	
YES	NO
Paula	Cassie
Vern	Brian
Michael	Tammy
Chris	Marge
Becky	Glenn
	Larry
	Ron
	Sandy

Pop to It!

Put popcorn to the test with this simple experiment. Collect two different brands of microwave popcorn and create a chart as shown. Ask youngsters to predict whether all the popcorn will pop and record their predictions on the chart. Then microwave one brand of popcorn according to the package directions. Pour the contents of the bag onto a large sheet of paper. Ask youngsters to sort the popcorn into two groups, popped and unpopped, and then discuss the results. If desired, extend the activity by instructing youngsters to count the two groups to see which has more. Repeat with a different brand of popcorn and compare the results. Ask youngsters to conclude which brand had more popped popcorn. Pop, pop, pop!

Body Beautiful

(Life Science)

Safety Skin

Demonstrate for youngsters how skin protects the body with this easy experiment. Fill two bowls with water, and then cover one bowl with plastic wrap to represent the skin. Ask a child to blow on the top of each bowl to represent wind. Ask another child to drip a few drops of blue food color onto each bowl to represent rain. Ask another child to sprinkle pepper onto each bowl to represent dirt and germs. Discuss and compare how the "skin" helps protect the water in one bowl. Guide youngsters to understand that their skin protects their bodies from weather, dirt, and germs.

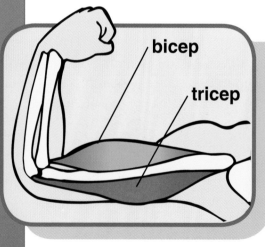

bicep

tricep

Muscles in Motion

Get youngsters moving to learn how muscles power their bodies with this simulation activity. You will need a red and a blue towel. To begin, ask each child to observe the muscles in his upper arm as he bends and then straightens his forearm. Explain that the bicep muscle pulls the upper forearm to bend the elbow and the tricep muscle pulls on the lower forearm to straighten the elbow. Then have one child represent the arm by standing with his hands resting on his shoulders. Place one end of each towel in his hands so that the red towel hangs on his back and the blue towel hangs in front of him as shown. Have one student be the bicep by holding the free end of the blue towel. Have another student be the tricep by holding the free end of the red towel. Ask the bicep to flex his muscle by pulling on the blue towel, making the arm bend forward. Then ask the tricep to pull on the red towel to straighten the arm again. Repeat the simulation until each child has had a turn. Flex, straighten, flex!

Follow That Cookie!

Use this simple model-making activity to help youngsters understand the digestive system journey that begins with one bite of food. In advance, draw a mouth on an index card, thread a button onto a 25-foot piece of yarn, and tape the yarn to the back of the card. Also obtain an illustration of the digestive system. Give each child a cookie to eat as you show the illustration. Discuss the functions of each part: the mouth (biting, chewing), esophagus (swallowing muscles move food down), stomach (muscles mix food with special juices), and intestines (muscles move liquid food to bloodstream and move wastes out). Then hold the card and have several students outstretch the yarn (have them spread out in the classroom if necessary). Tell youngsters that this is the length of the digestive tubes within their bodies. Ask several children to help push the button from the mouth to the end of the yarn. Compare the button to the cookie each child ate and then compare the children moving the button to the muscles that push food along every inch of our long digestive systems.

	We Predict	We Count
[cup]	Alex – 10 Ashley – 7 Jerry – 11 Cindy – 11	10
Milk	Alex – 10 Ashley – 7 Jerry – 11 Cindy – 11	5
Juice	Alex – 10 Ashley – 7 Jerry – 11 Cindy – 11	12

Liquid Life

From head to toes, life-giving blood flows—and youngsters may be amazed that their bodies carry about five pints of it! Help them visualize how much blood is in their bodies with this measurement activity. Collect a gallon-size plastic container labeled at five pints (ten cups), a funnel, an eight-ounce plastic cup, a clean pint-size milk carton, and a clean juice box with the top removed. You'll need a sink or plastic tub filled with water (tint with red food color if desired). Ask youngsters in a small group to predict how many of each container it will take to equal five pints. Record predictions on a chart as shown. Ask a child to fill the cup with water and use the funnel to pour the water into the labeled container. Have her refill the cup as many times as necessary to equal five pints as the group counts the number of cups. Record findings on the chart. Ask two other children to repeat the activity using the milk carton and the juice box. Discuss the results with youngsters.

5 pints

Fun Float and Sink

(Physical Science)

Harvest Float

Harvest youngsters' prediction skills with this fun float-and-sink discovery. In advance, gather Indian corn, squash, an apple, a pear, some unshelled nuts, and several sizes of pumpkins. (If any child is allergic to nuts, omit the nuts.) Place all the items in a basket beside your water table. Encourage children to examine each item and then predict which ones will float and which ones will sink. Then ask several students at a time to test each item. Record their findings on a chart as shown. Have youngsters sort the items into two groups: those that float and those that sink. If desired, use this activity as a center for further investigation.

	Float	Sink
big pumpkin	☺	☹
apple	☺	☹
little pumpkin		
pear		
squash		
Indian corn		
acorns		

Leaf Launch

Fallen leaves floating in a puddle—do they ever sink? Invite youngsters to investigate with this water table activity. To prepare, gather a supply of freshly fallen leaves; store the leaves in a plastic tub near your water table. Also gather several items to experiment with to try to sink the leaves (small rocks, blocks, metal washers, foam packing pieces, foam balls). Ask a child to place a leaf on the water and then use one hand to gently press it to the bottom of the table. Encourage youngsters to discuss why the leaf floats back to the surface of the water. Have the child push the leaf down again and then place some of the items on top of it to make the leaf sink. Ask youngsters to hypothesize why the leaf stays on the bottom now.

Rock the Boat

Nothing floats like a boat, and youngsters will discover just how much weight it takes to sink a boat with this experiment. Gather a plastic bowl, a plastic plate, an aluminum pie pan, and a supply of unshelled walnuts or small rocks. Ask a student to place the bowl, plate, and pie pan in a tub of water. Ask children to predict how many nuts or rocks it will take to sink each one. Have youngsters add nuts or rocks to each one until it begins to sink. Then count the number of nuts or rocks on each one and compare the findings to their predictions.

Floating Foil

Ahoy, mateys! Challenge youngsters' design skills as they make their own floatable foil boats. Give each child a sheet of aluminum foil, and set out a tub of water and the walnuts or rocks from "Rock the Boat" above. Ask each child to design and create a boat that will float in the water. Then ask him to predict how many nuts or rocks his boat will hold and record the number on a chart as shown. Encourage him to test his prediction by placing one nut or rock at a time on his boat. Have him count the nuts or rocks, record his findings, and compare them with his prediction. Smooth sailing!

	Predict	Count
Alex	9	8
Ashley	20	5
Jacob	8	7
Sophie	12	6
Karen	10	10
Seth	6	8
Jessie	11	9

Shape-Up

(Physical Science)

Great Growing Shapes

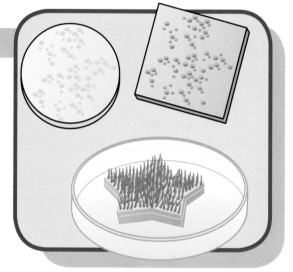

Watch youngsters' interest in shape recognition grow with this fun experiment. To prepare, cut different shapes from Swell Sponge sheets (flat, dry sponges found in craft stores), or use clean sponges that have been placed in a dryer for five minutes. You'll also need a small amount of grass seed. As youngsters observe, place each sponge in a shallow dish and then pour water into each dish. Discuss with youngsters why the sponges seem to grow as they absorb water. Then ask a child to sprinkle grass seed onto each sponge shape. Place each dish near a window and add water to keep the sponges moist. Have youngsters observe the sponges daily, and within a week great grassy growing shapes will appear!

Sandpaper Shapes

Texture adds fun to this small-group shape-making activity. To prepare, gather an 8½" x 11" sheet of sandpaper, a sheet of construction paper, several different-colored lengths of yarn and a magnifying glass for each child in a small group. Have each child place a piece of yarn on the construction paper and one on the sandpaper to test which type of paper the yarn will stick to. *(Fibers on the yarn will stick to the rough sandpaper and not to the smooth construction paper.)* Then have her observe each paper with the magnifying glass to see the rough texture of the sandpaper and the smooth texture of the construction paper. Ask her to use the yarn to make a circle, a square, a triangle, and a rectangle on the sandpaper. Encourage youngsters to create a scene using all four shapes as shown. Have youngsters share their creations with the group as they name each shape.

Magnificent Magnets

(Physical Science)

Sensory Table Snow

Engage your youngsters in this blizzard of activity involving magnetism. To prepare, gather a collection of magnetic and nonmagnetic items, such as large paper clips, milk jug lids, craft sticks, nuts and bolts, craft beads, and metal washers. Scatter these objects in the bottom of your sensory table. Then cover them with a layer of white Styrofoam packing pieces. Give each child who visits this center a magnet wand. Have her "dig" through the snow with her wand to find all the magnetic items. Once the items are retrieved, encourage her to hypothesize about why the magnet didn't pick up the remaining objects.

We're attracted to each other!

Sleigh Bells Ring?

Take the jingle out of the jingle bell with this magnetic exploration. Hold a jingle bell in one hand and ring it in front of your students. Then pick up the bell with a strong magnet. Hold the bell by the magnet, as shown, and gently shake it. There's no sound! The magnet attracts not only the outside of the bell but the inside as well! Stock your discovery center with different sizes of jingle bells and magnets for further exploration. Jingle all the way!

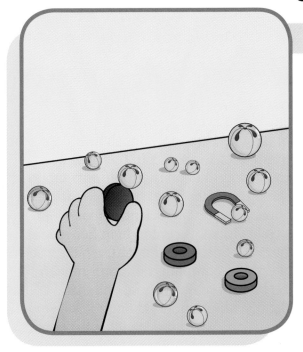

Fabulous Five Senses
(Life Science)

Sight

No Peeking!

After this activity, all eyes will be wide open to draw conclusions about the importance of the sense of sight. To prepare, provide a class supply of drawing paper and crayons. Ask each child in a small group to position a sheet of paper in front of himself and then choose a crayon. Instruct each child to close his eyes and try to draw a snowman on his paper—without peeking! (If desired, provide blindfolds for your students to use.) After a few minutes of drawing, have each child open his eyes and inspect his drawing. When the giggles die down, don't pass up this opportunity to discuss the importance of sight.

Sneaky Snowman

The eyes have it in this activity, which requires a keen sense of sight for a sweet reward. In advance, bring in several different pairs of shoes that have patterns on the soles. Also provide a bowl of holiday candy and a note similar to the one shown. Cut out several large, light blue footprint shapes. Use one pair of the shoes to make white-paint footprints on the footprint cutouts. During a center time, scatter the footprints around your science area. When a child visits this center, help her read the note. Encourage her to use her sense of sight to compare the footprint with the bottom of each shoe, and then identify which shoes belong to Sneaky Snowman. When she identifies the correct shoes, she gets a piece of candy!

Dear Children,

I left my footprints In your room so neat. If you can find my shoes, You may take a treat!

From,

Sneaky Snowman

Touch

Fancy Wraps

Wrap up these festive packages with a discriminating sense of touch! In advance, collect two samples each of a variety of textured items such as cotton, velvet, sandpaper, burlap, fur, and corduroy. Cut each textured item into equal-size squares. Glue one of each texture to a sheet of poster board and add a gift bow as shown. Put the remaining textured squares in a drawstring bag. To do this activity, have a child put her hand in the bag and isolate one of the squares. Encourage her to describe what she feels and then guess which package on the poster board is its match. Have her pull the square from the bag to check her guess. If she's right, she lays that square on top of its matching package. If not, she puts it back in the bag and tries again, repeating the process until each package has been matched. It's a wrap!

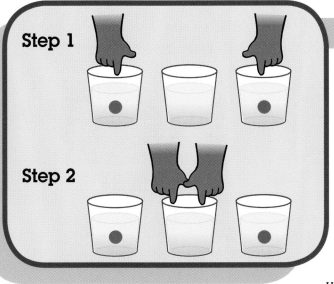

Step 1

Step 2

Hot or Cold to You?

This experiment will get those scientific minds going! For each small group of children, you'll need a cup of warm water, a cup of ice water, a cup of room-temperature water, one blue sticker, and one red sticker. Place the blue sticker on the cup of ice water and the red one on the warm water. In turn, ask each child to put his right index finger in the warm water and his left index finger in the cold water. After a minute or so, instruct him to dip both fingers in the room-temperature water. How does each finger feel? (Since the right finger was in the warm water for a while, it adjusted to that temperature. When placed in the room-temperature water, it felt cold. And the opposite is true for the left finger.)

Smell

Gingerbread Friends

There's a little matchmaking going on in this aromatic sorting center. In advance, cut out six gingerbread people from sandpaper. Then add details to each cutout with a permanent marker. Program the backs of every two cutouts with the same matching shape (for self-checking). Rub the front of each cutout with a glue stick. Then sprinkle ground cinnamon on the first set of matching gingerbread people. Sprinkle ground cloves on the second pair of cutouts. Finally, sprinkle the last two cutouts with ground ginger. After shaking off the excess spices, mix up the gingerbread friends and place them on a cookie sheet. Invite a child to use her sense of smell to match up the gingerbread friends. To check her work, she turns the cutouts over and looks for matching shapes.

pine

gingerbread

lemon

coffee

peppermint

sugar cookie

Seasonal Scents

Only the nose knows the secret to success in this activity. To prepare, gather a small collection of holiday candles that are strongly scented. For each candle, draw a picture of its scent on a different index card. Laminate the cards. To do this activity, invite a child to smell the candles and then match each candle to the picture of its scent.

Taste

The Tastery

It's time to sharpen up those taste buds! To prepare for this activity, draw a small picture of an apple on the rim of a paper plate. Draw a pear on the rim of a second plate and a banana on a third. Cover each picture by taping a flap of construction paper over it. (Tape only the top so it can be flipped up to reveal the picture underneath it.) Then peel and dice raw apples, pears, and bananas. Arrange each food on the corresponding plate. Invite children to guess which food is which from a short distance away (without smelling). Ask which sense they think they could use to check their guesses. Then have them taste each different food. After guessing, invite them to flip the flaps to check their guesses. (The sense of smell might also be used to help identify the foods.)

I predict I will like...

Chocolate	Chocolate-raspberry
Tasha	
Jordan	
Andrea	
Derek	Terry
Kalen	Allison
Ashley	Cody
Alex	Kastin

I tasted it! I like...

Chocolate	Chocolate-raspberry
	Andrea
Ashley	Tasha
Jordan	Terry
Derek	Allison
Cody	Kalen
Alex	Kastin

Taste Tempters

In this tempting activity, the taste buds declare their preferences! In advance, prepare two batches of instant hot chocolate: one regular and one with an added flavor such as raspberry. Prepare two two-column graphs that both reflect the hot chocolate flavors. To begin, ask students which flavor of hot chocolate they think they will like better. Have each child write his name on a sticky note and place it on the first graph to indicate his prediction. Then offer each child a taste of both hot chocolate flavors. Have each child write his name on another sticky note and place it on the second chart to indicate his actual preference. Which is the favorite? Is it the same as the predicted favorite? What sense did you use to determine your favorite flavor?

Hearing

Little Elf, Little Elf

Fine-tune the sense of hearing with a bit of help from those busy little elves. (Or substitute another theme to suit your curriculum.) Blindfold one student who will sit before your class and pose as Santa Claus. Then choose one child to approach the blindfolded Santa and knock on a door or table nearby. Have Santa say, "Little elf, little elf, why are you here?" Instruct the elf to reply, "I'm here to help you, Santa dear." Encourage Santa to use his sense of hearing to guess the name of the little elf. (If Santa needs to hear more, invite him to ask more questions of the elf.) When Santa guesses correctly, have the elf take Santa's place. Continue playing in the same manner until each child has had a turn to be Santa.

Jingle, Jingle

Can you tell where the jingle bell is—without looking? Let's see! To prepare for this game, seat a blindfolded child in the middle of a circle of children. Give a jingle bell to one student in the circle. At your signal, have the whole circle quietly walk around the room. As they walk, invite the bell holder to shake the bell. Encourage the blindfolded child to use her sense of hearing to keep track of where the bell is located. When you say, "Stop," have the circle of children and the bell shaking cease. Ask the blindfolded child to point to where she thinks the jingle bell is. How close did she get? How did she do that?

Nifty Nutrition
(Life Science)

"Nuttin'" but Delicious!

Chestnuts roasting on an open fire. Pecans and walnuts buried in holiday treats. Winter is full of opportunities to explore nuts. Not only do squirrels love them, but they make nutritious snacks for people, too. When eaten in limited quantities, nuts are a good source of protein. Some contain essential vitamins, such as A and E, while others can provide sources of iron and calcium.

Have parents send in a supply of nuts with shells. Hide them around the room while students are away. Then invite your little ones to scamper around to find the hidden treats. Once all of the nuts are found, explain their nutritional value and, if desired, crack open a few for students to snack on. (Be sure you check with parents first for any allergies before serving nuts to children.) Extend the learning by using the collection of nuts for some sorting and graphing practice. "Nut-tastic!"

Do you like dried or fresh fruit?	
Dried	Fresh
Logan	Quinn
Conner	Sara
Taylor	Hannah
Rylee	Brittany

Dried or Fresh?

Fruit is a nutritious snack any time of the year! But long ago people couldn't enjoy fresh fruit year-round. Explain to youngsters that early settlers had to dry pieces of fruit (remove the water from them) to preserve them and keep them from spoiling so that the fruit could be enjoyed during the winter. Gather some samples of dried fruit and their fresh counterparts, such as raisins and grapes, apples, bananas, and pineapple. Make a chart similar to the one shown. Then encourage youngsters to compare the tastes of the dried and fresh fruits, decide which they like better, and record their choices on the chart. Once everyone has had a turn, review the graph's results.

So Solid, Liquid, or Gas

(Physical Science)

Changes, Changes

Whether or not your area gets snow, your youngsters can still enjoy some frosty fun with this seasonal science observation. Have students use actual snow or a cooler of finely crushed ice to form a small snowman. Explain that snow and ice are solids. Set the figure on a piece of plywood or a cleared piece of sidewalk in the direct sun. Draw a chalk circle around the figure. Once the snowman starts to melt, explain that the solid is changing into a liquid. When it is completely melted, draw another circle around the puddle. Have youngsters compare the size difference between the two circles. Then allow more time to elapse before observing again. Look for the chalk circles to see that the puddle has disappeared. Explain to your little ones that the liquid evaporated, or changed into a gas, and was absorbed into the air. Cool!

Steamy!

What better way to observe a gas than to see steam rising from a fresh cup of hot cocoa! Bundle up and take a short walk outdoors with your youngsters. Have them identify any solids, liquids, or gases that they see. Point out smoke from a chimney (gas), air in a tire (gas), water puddles (liquid), or dirt in a planter (solid). After the walk, invite students to watch as you make a batch of cocoa. Explain that the powder is a solid. Add the hot, liquid water (or milk); then have your little ones watch the gassy steam rise into the air. Let the cocoa cool as youngsters draw a solid, a liquid, and a gas on paper. Then share this warm winter treat with everyone. Yum!

Get in Shape

So what shape is a liquid, anyway? Have your students ponder this question and encourage them to give you responses. Pour water into a bowl. Ask youngsters if a liquid is round. Now pour the water from the bowl into a 9" x 13" cake pan. Ask youngsters if a liquid is rectangular. Now explain to your students that one of the characteristics of a liquid is that it has no shape of its own. It always takes the shape of the container holding it. If desired, put a variety of containers at the water table for further exploration. So what shape is a liquid? No shape at all!

Move It!

Heat things up a bit in your classroom with this movement idea. Explain to your youngsters that all matter is made up of atoms. Atoms come together to form molecules. If the molecules are tightly packed together, the matter is a solid. If the molecules are moving and bouncing off one another, the matter is a liquid. If the molecules are moving really fast and far apart from one another, the matter is a gas.

Help demonstrate these ideas with your students. Gather a group of student "molecules" and have them stand still close together to resemble a solid. Next, have the students move away from one another and then walk around, intermingling in a limited area of space, to resemble a liquid. Finally, direct the children in the group to move faster and far apart from one another to resemble a gas. Solid is still, liquid is loose, and gas is on the go. Get the picture?

Incredible Ice

(Physical Science)

Icy Race

Which will melt first? Practice prediction skills with your youngsters as they observe the rate at which different forms of ice melt. In advance, fill one plastic cup with water and freeze it until solid. Use chart paper to prepare a class graph as shown. Next, fill a second cup with ice cubes and then fill a third cup with crushed ice. Place the three cups of ice on a table in front of your class. Ask youngsters to predict which cup of ice will melt first, second, and third. Discuss student responses; then record each student's guess for which will melt first. Ask youngsters to periodically observe the three cups of ice and compare the outcome with their predictions. Chillin'!

Which Will Melt First?		
		Shandi
	Kinsey	Jesse
Sophie	Ashley	Kastin
Kalen	Jacob	Alex
frozen solid	ice cubes	crushed ice

I came in second!

Magic Color Ice

Explore the magic of color mixing with ice! Prepare three bowls of colored salt water—red, yellow, and blue. You'll also need an eyedropper, a shallow container, and an ice cube. Place the ice cube in the container. Then use an eyedropper to add drops of the colored water (from two of the bowls, such as yellow and blue) to the top of the ice cube. Your little scientists will be amazed as the colors penetrate and mix to make a new color. Wow, magic ice!

Meltdown

Tiptoe into practicing prediction skills with this chilly activity. Discuss with children what it feels like to walk barefoot on a sidewalk as compared to the grass on a hot day. Now have them imagine a cold winter's morning. Would youngsters rather walk on a tile floor or on carpet? Lead them to conclude that different surfaces can have different temperatures. Have your children choose three different outdoor surfaces, such as a plastic slide, a wooden picnic bench, and the sidewalk. Encourage youngsters to predict on which surface an ice cube would melt quickest. Then place an ice cube on each surface and have youngsters check each one periodically to observe melting. And the great meltdown winner is...

I'm winning!

Frosty!

Get that frosty-mug sensation as your little ones create these frosty art projects. In advance, collect a mug, Epsom salts, several paintbrushes, and a class supply of dark blue construction paper. To prepare, trace a large mug pattern on each piece of paper and place the real mug in the freezer. Explain to youngsters that frost is a pattern of ice crystals that forms when water vapor freezes. Tell them that frost normally occurs outdoors on chilly days. Show youngsters the mug and have them observe the frost that has formed on it. Then give each child a sheet of construction paper and have them watch as you mix one cup of Epsom salts with one-half cup of hot water. Stir until the salt has dissolved. Then invite each child to paint the mixture over his mug tracing and let it dry. If desired, provide cotton balls, red pom-poms, and glue for him to embellish his mug to resemble an ice-cream float as shown. When the creations are dry, have each child cut his out. Display all the mugs on a bulletin board titled "Frosty Sensations."

Think Thermometers
(Physical Science)

Up and Down

Use this demonstration with a small group of students to introduce how a thermometer works. Prepare a cup of icy water, a cup of hot water, and a cup of lukewarm water. (For safety reasons do not allow youngsters to touch the hot water.) Show youngsters a thermometer. Explain that a thermometer is a tool that measures temperature, or how hot or cold something is. Have children brainstorm a list of different things that are hot or cold. Then place the thermometer in the cup of lukewarm water. Explain that the liquid inside the thermometer will go up or down depending on the temperature. Read the temperature of the water. Now stick the thermometer into the icy water. Direct children to observe what happens to the liquid inside the thermometer. The water is cold so the liquid goes down to lesser numbers. Have students predict what will happen when the thermometer goes into the hot water. Will the liquid go up or down? Put the thermometer in the hot water to test the predictions. Follow up by changing the thermometer between the hot and cold water to reinforce the concept.

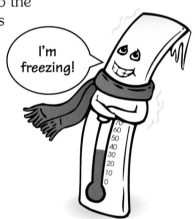

I'm freezing!

These places have different temperatures:

Jacob, Sophie–	window, clozit
Alex, Ashley–	sink wotr, wotr fontin
Jerry, Cindy–	sidwok, Under tree

Temperature Explorations

Now that your youngsters have a feel for what a thermometer does, encourage them to explore and experiment on their own. Provide each pair of students with a thermometer. Have them find two places in the classroom (or outdoors) that are different temperatures. (You may need to give hints about the coolness of shade and the heat of the sun.) Have each pair record the different locations on a class chart similar to the one shown. If desired, also have them write the temperatures on the chart. Cool!

Shadow Show

(Physical Science)

Shadow Sizes

Put a little problem solving into shadow fun with this illuminating idea. Draw several squares of different sizes on your chalkboard. Cut out a tagboard square and tape it to a craft stick. Give the square cutout and a flashlight to a pair of students. Have them work together to make the square's shadow fit each of the outlines on the board. What happens when the cutout moves closer to the flashlight? It gets bigger! For a winter flair, use a hand cutout and glove outlines or a bear cutout and cave outlines. "Shadow-rific"!

A "Hole" Lot of Shadows!

Here's a demonstration to help youngsters learn more about shadows. Position your overhead projector or a large flashlight six feet away from a wall. Gather your students around and then hold a 3" x 5" index card about a foot from the wall so that it makes a rectangular shadow. Punch a hole near the center of the card and hold it up again so that students can see the new shadow. Ask a volunteer to cover the hole with her finger; then discuss the shadow change. Have students infer what makes the hole in the shadow appear and disappear. Then watch your little ones beam as they discover that the hole appears in the shadow when light is able to pass through the hole in the card.

Heart Healthy
(Life Science)

Heartbeat Challenge

Squeeze in some knowledge about the human heart with this activity. Divide your students into groups of three. Give each group a one-minute timer and a small foam or rubber ball that can be squeezed. Designate one child in each group to be the timer, another child to be the counter, and the last child to be the heart.

On the timer's signal, the heart "beats" as many times as she can in one minute. The heart beats by squeezing the ball. The counter keeps track of the heartbeats. After one minute, have members in the groups change roles. Continue until each child has had a turn to do all three jobs. Did any heart beat 60–100 times? That's how many times our resting hearts beat every minute of every hour of every day. Whew!

I beat!

to body   to lungs

used blood from body

blood full of oxygen from lungs

Go With the Flow

Youngsters now know that the heart beats constantly and rather quickly. But why does the heart beat? To move blood through the body! Invite your students to be the blood to help demonstrate how it flows through the heart. To prepare, tape a large human heart cutout to the floor as shown. On the wrists of half of your children, tie lengths of red crepe paper (to represent oxygenated blood). On the wrists of the other half of your students, tie lengths of blue crepe paper (to represent blood without oxygen).

Explain to youngsters that there are two ways for blood to enter and leave the heart. Blood travels from the lungs into the heart to be pumped out to the body so that it can take oxygen to the body parts. The "used" blood (without oxygen) then comes back into the heart to be pumped to the lungs to receive more oxygen. Use the diagram above to move your little ones through the heart to model blood flow. (If desired, play music as youngsters walk.) Go, blood, go!

Terrific Teeth
(Life Science)

Bye-Bye, Baby Teeth

Set up this tactile center so that your youngsters can model how permanent teeth replace baby teeth. In advance, gather play dough, ten small craft sticks cut in half, and five large craft sticks cut in half. Demonstrate for youngsters how to mold two pieces of play dough into two thick semicircles as shown. Tell students these represent the upper and lower gums in the mouth. Have youngsters help push the small craft sticks into the play dough to represent 20 baby teeth as shown. Then press a larger stick (representing a permanent tooth) through the gum so that it pushes a smaller stick out and replaces it. Explain to students that they have permanent teeth in their gums and in time those will replace their baby teeth. Then place the gums and teeth at a center for little tooth fairies to practice counting and replacing baby teeth.

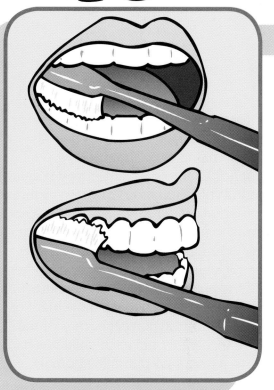

Little ones have 20 baby teeth.

That's the Way It Goes!

To reinforce good dental health, invite your youngsters to pantomime brushing their teeth properly as you sing this song together.

(sung to the tune of "Pop! Goes the Weasel")

Brush back and forth on chewing teeth.
Everybody knows
For healthy teeth and happy teeth,
That's the way it goes!

On inner and outer surfaces,
Make angled strokes just so.
For healthy teeth and happy teeth,
That's the way it goes!

Homey Habitats

(Life Science)

A Cozy Cricket Cottage

Invite youngsters to help you create a cricket haven so that they can enjoy the sights and sounds of these interesting little insects. Buy a few crickets from your local bait shop or pet store. Bring the crickets, along with a clear plastic jar (with holes in the lid for air), into the classroom. Then take your students outdoors to collect a few twigs, dried leaves, grass, and soil. Put a layer of soil in the container; then add the other objects. Now you're ready to put the crickets into their new habitat. Have youngsters observe the habitat and record their observations through pictures and writing. Mist the habitat with water daily and add a piece of raw potato for the crickets to eat. If desired, share the facts listed below with youngsters.

The cricket sits on a lef.

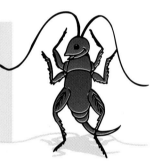

- Crickets are relatives of grasshoppers and katydids.
- Only male crickets chirp.
- Crickets chirp more frequently in warmer weather.
- Crickets hear with their legs.
- A female field cricket lays up to 200 eggs at one time.
- A cricket chirps by rubbing its wings together.

desert

camel

forest

shark

lizard

squ octop bear

ocean

frog

pond

Home Hunting

Here's a fun follow-up activity for reinforcing the different types of animal homes. Label each corner of your room with the name of a different environment (for example, desert, forest, ocean, pond). Write the names or draw pictures of different animals that live in these environments on separate paper strips and place them in a bag. Have one child at a time pick a strip from the bag. Help her read the animal name; then encourage her to mimic this animal's movement as she heads for the correct corner of the room. Continue until each child has had a turn. There's no place like home!

Sassy Seeds
(Life Science)

Seed Secrets

Invite little detectives to solve some seed secrets as they practice sorting and classification skills. To prepare, place seeds from various fruits on a paper plate. On another paper plate, place a slice of each corresponding fruit with the seed side down (make sure the fruit slice still contains some seeds). Give a small group of youngsters a magnifying glass to inspect each seed. Encourage them to discuss the size and shape of each seed and compare that to each fruit. Then ask them to predict which seed belongs with which fruit. To check, have them turn each fruit slice over and match seeds.

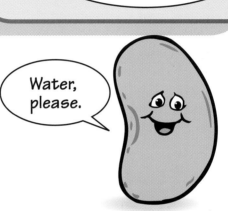

Water, please.

Seedy Growth

What do seeds need to grow? Set up this experiment for junior scientists to observe how well seeds grow with different liquids. To prepare, collect four clear plastic cups, soil, four lima beans, soda, juice, water, and coffee. Remind youngsters that plants need air, light, and water to grow. Explain that when sprouting seeds indoors electrical light can replace sunlight. Investigate to determine if seeds will sprout when water is replaced with other liquids. Ask a small group to help plant four seeds in four separate soil cups, placing each seed against the side of the cup as shown. Label each cup with the word (water, soda, juice, or coffee). Then add each liquid to its corresponding cup. Have students observe the seeds daily and add liquid as needed. Compare the growth of each seed. Discuss with youngsters why some liquids may prevent or slow seed growth. (Soda and coffee contain chemicals; juice contains acid.)

Plenty of Plants

(Life Science)

Alive or Not?

Introduce youngsters to the concepts of living and nonliving things with this classification activity. Collect various objects (such as buttons, marbles, rocks, real flowers, a carrot, a small plant) and place them in a plastic container. (For this activity toy animals and similar items could be used to represent living things.) Create a recording chart as shown and lay it on a table. Discuss with youngsters what living things need to survive *(air, water, food).* Invite a child to remove one object from the container and decide if it is a living or a nonliving thing. Encourage her to give reasons for her answer. Then have her place the object on the correct section of the chart. Repeat until all objects have been classified.

Seeds and More

Perk up prediction skills as youngsters observe different types of plant growth with this experiment. To prepare, collect three clear plastic jars (two with lids), a slice of bread, several lima beans (soaked in water overnight), construction paper, an onion, and cotton balls. Have students observe the bread, the beans, and the onion and ask them to predict which one will grow a new plant. *(All will sprout from spores, seeds, or a bulb.)* Then set up three experiments with youngsters' assistance. First, place the bread inside a jar, add a few drops of water, replace the lid, and place the jar in a warm place. (In a few days mold will grow from spores.) Next, fill a jar with cotton, add water until the cotton is damp, and place the beans between the side of the jar and the cotton as shown. Replace the lid. To darken the jar, tape construction paper around it and then place it in a warm area. (In a few days remove the cover to view sprouts from the beans.) Finally, put an onion, root side down, in the jar of water with no lid and place it in a sunny window. (In a few days a sprout will grow from the bulb.) Continue to add water as necessary to observe further growth.

Favorite Vegetable

How Does Your Garden Grow?

Share *Growing Vegetable Soup* by Lois Ehlert to get youngsters thinking about plants and to create a class graph. After reading the story, give each child a sticky note and ask her to draw and color her favorite vegetable. Have each child hold up her illustration for all to view. Discuss the vegetables chosen and then sort the choices into separate vegetable groups. Have youngsters in each vegetable group sit together. Ask each child in each group, in turn, to place her note on a separate column of the graph as shown. Have one child at a time count the total for each different vegetable. Then discuss which vegetable represents the most and which the fewest on the graph.

Vote for ME!

Dandy Dirt

Your little gardeners will dig this hands-on small-group investigation. To prepare, gather several plastic sifters; then mix together potting soil, sand, crushed leaves, bits of clay, tiny twigs, small plastic bugs, and tiny stones in a large plastic tub. You'll also need a package of seeds and a class supply of small plastic cups. Invite several students to sift through the mixture to determine the individual ingredients of dirt. Explain that dirt found outdoors may contain tiny bits of dead plants and animals. Then stir the mixture so another group can investigate it. Later invite each child to pour sifted dirt into his cup and plant a seed. Have him add water and then place the cup in a sunny window. Encourage youngsters to check their mini garden daily and add water when needed.

Amazing Animals
(Life Science)

Real or Pretend?

Your little critters will enjoy this sound-making game as they practice critical-thinking skills. Read *While You Were Sleeping* by John Butler to youngsters to show them animals in their natural habitats. Then ask students to listen as you name a pretend animal (such as the Big Bad Wolf) or a real animal (such as a tiger). If the animal named is real, ask youngsters to make its sound. If the animal is a pretend animal, ask each child to place a finger over his mouth. To vary this activity, show children a picture of a real or a pretend animal (such as pictures from storybooks and picture calendars).

Can You Camouflage?

Teach youngsters how some animals hide from predators with this small-group game. In advance, collect several different-colored objects that match the color of things in your classroom (for example, a red counting chip that matches a red rug). Discuss with students how some animals use *camouflage* to survive (using the color of their skin, fur, or feathers to blend into the area around them). Show the group an object. Then ask one child to close her eyes while another child hides the object in a designated area of the classroom. Have the first child open her eyes and search for the object. If she has difficulty locating the hidden object, ask another child to give verbal clues until she finds it. Continue until each child in the group has had a turn to find an object. Compare the way in which the objects were hard to spot against a same-color background to the way some animals hide to be safe from predators searching for food.

Caterpillar Crunch

Youngsters will move to a butterfly beat and practice gross-motor skills with this life cycle exercise. Show youngsters an illustration of a caterpillar, a chrysalis, and a butterfly, and discuss the changes that occur during metamorphosis. If desired, read *From Caterpillar to Butterfly* by Deborah Heiligman to students. Then have each child find a space on the floor. Ask one child to model each life cycle action as you say each of these words: *caterpillar* (crawl on the floor pretending to munch on leaves), *chrysalis* (curl into a ball and pretend to sleep), *butterfly* (pretend to flutter wings). Ask all students to act out the life cycle as you repeat each word. Then play some music and ask youngsters to act out each phase in the correct order, changing positions as you randomly interrupt the music.

Bat Blinders

Youngsters will go batty over this simulation activity as they learn how bats use their senses. Ask youngsters to share what they know about bats. If desired, record their answers on chart paper. Explain to students that bats usually fly at night and depend on their keen sense of hearing to find food. (The bat makes sounds that bump up against objects, like trees and insects, then bounce back to the bat. This is called *echolation*.) Then have youngsters stand in a circle. Blindfold one child and have him stand in the center of the circle to represent the bat. Ask youngsters to remain quiet. Then point to one student and have her clap her hands. Have the blindfolded child use his sense of hearing to point in the direction of the clapping. Repeat until each child has had a turn to be the bat.

Living Large
(Life Science)

Bloomin' Knowledge

Get youngsters thinking about similarities and differences between living and nonliving things with this observation activity. To prepare, draw a Venn diagram on a sheet of paper and place a real potted plant and an artificial plant nearby as shown. Have youngsters observe each plant. Ask them to name ways the two plants are alike and ways they are different. Record students' answers on the diagram. Guide youngsters to conclude that the potted plant is living (needs air, water, and food to grow and change) and the other plant is nonliving.

Real Plant — **Artificial Plant**

needs dirt
short
needs water
wilts
needs light
breaks easily
smells

leaves
flowers
need containers
pretty

stiff
tall
stays the same
won't break
doesn't smell

1. It's green.
2. It needs water.
3. It's living.

Clue In

Little detectives will improve communication and critical-thinking skills when they clue in classmates with this guessing game. The day before this activity, give each child a paper bag to take home, and ask her to find an item to place in the bag. Ask parents to help their child write on the outside of the bag whether the item represents a living or nonliving thing. Also ask them to write two clues to help identify the item. (For this activity toy animals, dolls, and similar items should be used to represent living things.) Gather youngsters and have each child take turns reading her clues to the group. Encourage youngsters to guess the contents of each bag and tell why it represents a living or a nonliving thing.

Terrific Trees

Help youngsters compare seasonal trees with this unique art activity. Gather a class supply of 9" x 12" construction paper, colored tissue paper, paper tubes (or brown construction paper taped in a tube shape), brown yarn, beads, and popped popcorn. If possible, have children observe a real tree outside your classroom and discuss why it is a living thing. Then show youngsters seasonal pictures of one tree and discuss why it looks different during winter than it does during spring, summer, or fall. *(Trees may have a dormant, or nongrowing, period in wintertime because there is less water and sunlight. In springtime ice and snow melt to provide water, and there is more sunlight so these trees begin to grow again.)* Then give each child the supplies to create two different seasonal trees as shown. Help each child write the season below each of her trees. Display the "tree-mendous" creations for all to enjoy.

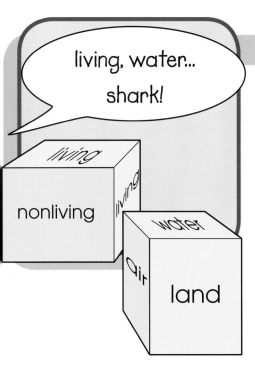

Roll 'Em!

Roll in a fun review of the concepts of living and nonliving things with this small-group game. To prepare, cover two separate tissue box cubes with solid-colored Con-Tact paper. Label one cube with the words *water, land,* and *air* (two sides each). Label the other cube with the words *living* and *nonliving* (three sides each) as shown. Review the words with youngsters. To play the game, have one child roll both cubes and help him read the words that are facing up. Ask him to name a plant, an animal, or an object that fits the descriptive words. Continue to play until each child has had a turn. As a variation, glue pictures on each cube to illustrate each word. Give it a roll!

41

Great Growth and Change
(Life Science)

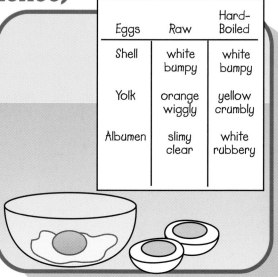

Eggs	Raw	Hard-Boiled
Shell	white bumpy	white bumpy
Yolk	orange wiggly	yellow crumbly
Albumen	slimy clear	white rubbery

"Egg-citing" Exploration

Investigate changes in form with this egg comparison activity. You'll need one hard-boiled egg and a plastic knife for each small group of students, a small clear bowl, and a raw chicken egg. Prepare a recording chart as shown. If desired, have *The Egg* by Gallimard Jeunesse available to use as a picture reference. Show youngsters the raw egg and then crack it open into the bowl. (For safety, do not allow any child to touch the raw egg or eggshell). Invite youngsters to observe the egg and discuss the parts of the egg (shell, yolk, and *albumen,* or egg white). Encourage them to describe each part of the raw egg and record their answers on the chart as shown. Have each small group peel a hard-boiled egg, slice it in half, and observe the inside of it. Ask youngsters to describe each part of the boiled egg and record their responses. Review the chart and compare the similarities and differences of the two forms of the egg. Challenge youngsters to hypothesize what happened to make the change in the egg.

Handy Height

Handy Height

Susan —

Austin —

Kalen —

Help youngsters keep track of their growth with this handy height chart. In advance, collect a five-foot sheet of bulletin board paper and tempera paint. To make a nonstandard measurement growth chart, ask each child to press a handprint onto the paper as shown. After it dries, display the chart on a wall. Then invite pairs of youngsters to help each other measure by counting how many hands tall each stands. Have each pair record heights by drawing lines on the chart and writing corresponding names. Revisit the chart monthly to help youngsters compare their growth.

Air All Around

(Earth Science)

Air Art

Feel a soft springtime breeze? Youngsters will find out what a little moving air can do with this colorful experiment. In advance, put out several different colors of tempera paint, and gather a class supply of straws and white paper. Give each child a straw and ask him to blow into it to experiment with moving different objects (paper, a pencil, etc.) around on a table. Then put a small amount of each color of paint onto each child's paper. Have him blow into the straw to move the paint around on his paper. Encourage him to create a shape by blowing the paint in different directions. Display the creations on a bulletin board titled "Airy Art."

Air, Air, Everywhere!

Help youngsters understand that air is all around them with these three quick and easy experiments. Collect a two-liter plastic bottle, a balloon, and a class supply of resealable plastic bags. Show children the uncapped empty bottle and ask them to describe what is in it. Now squeeze the bottle onto their hands so they can feel the air rushing out of it. Discuss with students that air is all around even though we cannot see it, smell it, or taste it. Next, blow up a balloon and allow youngsters to feel it. (For safety reasons, do not allow them to play with the balloon.) Release the air from the balloon as youngsters feel the air escaping and listen to the sound from it. Discuss how the shape of the balloon changes when the air is released. Challenge children to "catch" air inside a plastic bag, reseal it, and press gently on the bag to feel the air inside. Air is here and there; it's everywhere!

Wondrous Weather
(Earth Science)

Changing Weather, Changing Clothes

Improve thinking skills as youngsters sort out which type of clothing is best for each seasonal weather change. Collect several pieces of clothing to represent each season (raincoat, jacket, mittens, hats, swimsuit, boots, etc.) and place them in a bag. Create a graph as shown and collect a class supply of index cards. Pull one piece of clothing from the bag at a time and ask youngsters to help sort them by season. Discuss with youngsters why it is important to wear appropriate seasonal clothing. Have each child choose one piece of clothing and illustrate it on an index card. Then have each child tape her card in the correct column on the graph.

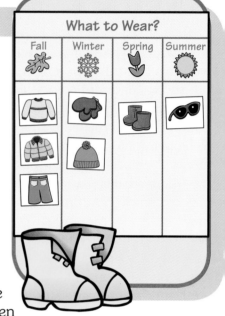

What to Wear?			
Fall	Winter	Spring	Summer

Time	Direction
8:00	S
10:00	E
12:00	S

Windy-Weather Watchers

Help youngsters learn directions as they flutter through this windy experiment. In advance, make four signs with directions printed on them (north, south, east, west) and cut a class supply of 18-inch pieces of ribbon. Create a chart as shown. Tape the four signs onto four different students and tie a piece of ribbon on the wrists of all other students. Take the class outside on a windy day and position the students with signs (if desired, have youngsters help using a simple compass). Have the other students stand with their ribbon arms extended. Ask youngsters to observe which way the ribbons are blowing to determine the wind direction. Record the time and wind direction on the chart. Repeat the experiment several times during the day (or at the same time the next day) to see if the wind direction changes.

Drip, Drip, Drop

Simulate for youngsters how a cloud holds many water droplets that combine to make a rain shower. To prepare, place a piece of white felt over an open jar and secure it with a rubber band to represent a cloud. You'll also need an eyedropper. Begin dripping water onto the felt cloud as youngsters help count the droplets. Be careful not to bump the table. If desired, have youngsters take turns carefully adding droplets to the cloud. Continue adding water droplets until the cloud is so full of water that it begins to drip into the jar. Drip, drip, drop a little rain shower!

Foggy Jar

Use this small-group demonstration to help youngsters understand how fog forms. In advance, collect a glass jar with a small opening (so an ice cube can sit on top of it without falling into the jar), ice cubes, and hot water. For safety, keep all youngsters away from the hot water. Gather a small group of students and place the jar in a sunny window. Pour hot water into the jar until it is about one-third full. Carefully place an ice cube on the jar opening. Have youngsters observe as the warm air from the water meets the cold air from the ice cube and fog forms in the jar. Discuss with youngsters how this experiment compares to fog seen outside on a chilly morning.

Curious Clouds

(Earth Science)

Yummy Clouds

Fluffy, flat, or feathery—help youngsters identify different types of clouds with this sweet activity. In advance, collect a class supply of resealable plastic bags, blue plastic plates, and several tubs of whipped cream. To prepare, half-fill each bag with whipped cream, press out the air, and reseal each one. Share pictures of the three main types of clouds (cumulus: puffy, cottonlike; stratus: flat, thick blankets; cirrus: curly white). If desired, share *The Cloud Book* by Tomie dePaola with youngsters. Then give each child a plate and a bag. Snip off one corner of each bag. Ask each child to gently squeeze the bag to form a cloud on his plate. Invite him to use his fingers to form puffy, curly, or flat clouds. Challenge him to compare his cloud with the cloud illustrations and then identify each type. Finally, invite each child to eat his yum, yum, yummy cloud.

I'm a cumulus cloud!

Kastin

Cottony Clouds

Here's a relaxing observation activity that will get youngsters' imaginations rolling. You'll need a package of cotton balls and a class supply of light blue construction paper. On a warm, cloudy day take your class outside to cloud-gaze. Encourage youngsters to identify different shapes they see in the clouds. Return to your classroom and have youngsters recreate one cloud shape using cotton balls. Model how to gently pull apart each cotton ball to make different shapes. Then have each child glue her cottony cloud onto her paper. If desired, help youngsters identify the cloud type using the information from "Yummy Clouds" above.

Wheelin' Round

(Physical Science)

Wonderful Wheels

Let youngsters investigate how a simple machine can make work easier with this movement experiment. In advance, gather a large bag of potting soil, a cardboard box, and several cylindrical wooden blocks (or same-size soup cans). Show youngsters how difficult it is to move the bag of soil by dragging it across the classroom floor. Ask them to brainstorm ways that would make it easier to move the bag. Place the bag inside the box and ask a child to move it, pointing out that it is a little easier to move this time. Ask youngsters to explore different ways to use the blocks or cans to move the bag. Guide them to see that placing the blocks underneath the box with the bag inside would make the job very easy. Compare this experiment to the wheels on wheelbarrows and wagons that make movement easier.

Let's roll!

Freewheelin'

Put a scientific spin on biking with this revolving measurement investigation. You'll need a bicycle, yarn, and colored tape. Place a piece of tape on one wheel of the bike and a piece of tape on the floor. Position the bike so the tape marks are aligned as shown. Ask youngsters to predict how far the bicycle will travel with one full turn of the tire. Then have each child cut a length of yarn to match her guess. Ask one child to slowly roll the bike forward until the tape mark makes one complete revolution. Encourage youngsters to watch the tape on the tire as it makes one revolution. Mark the distance traveled by placing another piece of tape on the floor. Then have each child check her prediction by laying her yarn between the tape marks on the floor. If desired, place other toys with wheels in a center for youngsters to practice further. How moving!

Soil Samples

(Earth Science)

Earthy Examination

Dig into nitty-gritty soil exploration as youngsters improve communication skills. To prepare, fill four separate plastic tubs with different types of earthy material (potting soil, sand, gravel, playground soil). Also gather several plastic sieves, magnifying glasses, glue, and an 8½" x 11" sheet of poster board for each small group. Invite each group to investigate each sample with a magnifying glass and by sifting each with a sieve. Encourage them to discuss the color, texture, and scent of each sample. Have the group glue a small amount of each sample onto a section of the poster board as shown. Help them write descriptive words for each sample. Later, have each group share their soil description posters with the class.

potting soil	playground soil
dark chunky	dusty tan
sand	gravel
dry scratchy	rocky hard

I'm rich!

All Soaked Up

Youngsters will soak up scientific-process skills with this soil absorbency experiment. To prepare, gather two eight-ounce clear plastic cups, one half cup each of dry soil and gravel, water, and a tablespoon. Show youngsters the soil and gravel, and then pour each into a separate clear cup. Ask youngsters to predict how many tablespoons of water each one will absorb. Record youngsters' predictions on a chart. Then pour one tablespoon of water into the soil as youngsters observe. Discuss why the water soaks into the soil. Continue adding one tablespoon of water at a time as youngsters observe and count. Stop when the soil is fully saturated (water stays on top of the surface). Record the final number of tablespoons. Repeat the process with the cup of gravel. Compare the final totals and discuss why the soil absorbed more water. *(Dry soil is made up of small particles that absorb water; gravel is made up of larger, hard particles that are less absorbent.)*

Creative Conservation
(Earth Science)

Recycled Toys

Teach your little conservationists about recycling as they use their imaginations to create a new toy. In advance, ask parents to send in recyclable materials (such as cereal boxes, paper towel tubes, plastic jugs, juice can lids, string, etc.). You'll also need tape or glue. Explain that *recycling* means "using something in a different way instead of throwing it away," and that recycling helps reduce pollution. Then invite youngsters to choose several items to tape or glue together to create a new toy. Invite each child to share her creation with the class. Display the toys on a table in the hallway for all to enjoy.

Recycle please!

Recycle Relay

Youngsters will race to this sorting activity as they learn about recycling. In advance, collect three different-colored plastic tubs and various clean, unbreakable recyclables (plastic jugs, aluminum cans, newspapers, paper bags, plastic bags, cardboard, etc.). Label each tub with an illustration of one type of recyclable (plastic jug, newspaper, can). As a group, sort the items by type (plastics, papers, aluminum), placing each in the corresponding bin. Then place all the items in one box and set up the relay as shown. To begin, give the first person in line one recyclable item; he races to the bins and places it in the correct bin. He returns and taps the next person in line. Continue until each child has had a turn. For a more challenging activity, set up two relay lines and have two teams race at once.

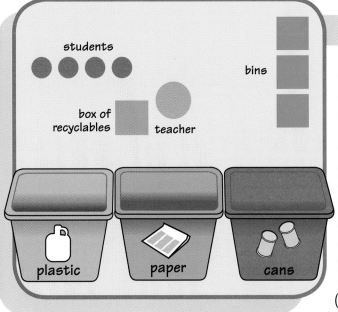

Bubblin' Up

(Physical Science)

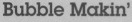

Bubble Makin'

Exploration is the name of the game with this bubbly activity. Gather several items that will make bubbles (such as a colander, a spool, and a funnel) and some that may not make bubbles (such as a spoon, a spatula, and a plastic fork). Set several pans of bubble solution outside with the collected items. Ask youngsters to predict which items they think will make bubbles. Then have youngsters sort the items into two groups—those that will make bubbles and those that will not. Invite youngsters to take turns trying to blow bubbles using each item. Afterward, have students sort the items again, making any needed changes among the two groups. Conclude the activity by discussing with youngsters the common attributes of the items that made bubbles (for example, those that have flat surfaces with small openings).

Bubbly Shapes

Are bubbles always round? Youngsters will enjoy discovering the answer with this experiment. To prepare, gather a class supply of pipe cleaners, plastic bubble wands (different shapes), and bubble solution. Begin by blowing bubbles over youngsters and discussing the shape and size of the bubbles. Ask youngsters to hypothesize if the bubble shape will change when the bubble wand shape changes. Give each child a pipe cleaner. Ask her to create a shaped bubble wand (heart, square, triangle, etc.) by bending the pipe cleaner. Then have one child at a time experiment with her bubble wand as the class observes. Discuss the shape of each bubble wand and compare it to the shape of the bubbles it creates. *(There is a force known as surface tension on the inside of the bubble as well as the outside of the bubble that pulls it into its round shape.)*

Burstin' Bubbles

Pop, pop, pop! Youngsters will have a blast popping bubbles to complete this color-mixing activity. For each group, prepare two separate bubble solutions, each tinted with a different primary food coloring (red, yellow, or blue). To begin the activity, take youngsters outside and divide them into small groups. Give each group one sheet of white poster board, a container of each tinted bubble solution, and bubble wands. Ask youngsters to dip the wands and blow bubbles onto the poster board. Have them observe where two different-colored bubbles burst near each other to form a new color on the poster board. Encourage youngsters to continue blowing bubbles until the poster board is full of bubble prints. Later, cut out large circles from each poster board creation and display them on the bubble bulletin board as shown in the activity below.

Bubble Board

Youngsters will practice observation and communication skills as they help create this bubbly display. In advance, collect a class supply of different-sized clear plastic lids, different-colored permanent markers, and chart paper. Have youngsters observe as one child blows a stream of bubbles into the air. Ask youngsters to describe the bubbles as you record their responses on the chart. Then give each child one plastic lid and a colored permanent marker. Direct her to write one word from the chart on her "bubble." Display all the bubbles on a bulletin board, along with the circles from the activity above. Title the board "Bubblin' Up!"

Interesting Insects

(Life Science)

Sniffing Out Snacks

Invite your little ones to be hungry ants in this sensory experience. Ahead of time, pick out two or three distinctive food extracts, such as lemon, peppermint, or vanilla. Saturate a different set of ten cotton balls with each scent. Create a path for each scent using tape to secure the cotton across a table or the floor. If desired, provide more of a challenge by having the paths of two different scents cross each other. Place a container of jelly beans that correspond to each scent at the end of each path. Explain to your students that ants smell with their antennae and that they use their sense of smell to search for food. Divide your youngsters into small groups. Assign each group to one of the scent paths so they can sniff their way to snacktime!

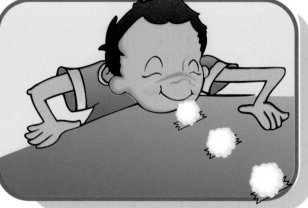

Insect	Wings	Three Body Sections	Six Legs	Antennae	Stinger
Ant	some	✓	✓	✓	
Grasshopper	✓	✓	✓	✓	some
Ladybug	✓	✓	✓	✓	
Wasp	✓	✓	✓	✓	
Fly	✓	✓	✓	✓	✓
Dragonfly	✓	✓	✓	✓	

Insect Study

Classification and comparison skills are put to the test here as youngsters work to record attributes of different insects. To prepare, read a nonfiction book about insects, such as *Bugs! Bugs! Bugs!* (Eyewitness Readers) by Jennifer Dussling. Then make a chart similar to the one shown, listing in the top spaces several different insect attributes. Next, have your students pick six different insects from the book to fill in the left side of the chart. Then discuss each insect's characteristics and have different students check the appropriate boxes. (Have several more insect reference books on hand in case additional research is needed.) Discuss the completed chart and help youngsters determine the main attributes of an insect *(six legs; three main body parts—head, thorax, and abdomen)*. Just buggy!

Insect Parts

Youngsters will enjoy this catchy tune, which helps reinforce the basic parts of an insect.

Display a large picture that shows the main parts of an insect. With each round of singing, have a different volunteer use a pointer to identify the insect parts as they are sung.

(sung to the tune of "Shoo Fly")

Head, thorax, abdomen,
Head, thorax, abdomen,
Head, thorax, abdomen,
Two antennae and six legs!

Grass Hopping

Name	Prediction	Actual
Greg	20	50
Sarina	10	62
Brittany	80	78
Jon	5	69
Dennis	217	98
Heather	25	101
Jaden	100	88

Grass Hopping

Grasshoppers can jump about 20 times their body length. Can your little ones? Challenge each student to use his estimating, counting, recording, and measurement skills to predict how many jumps it would take him to jump 20 times the length of his body. Begin by measuring a child with yarn; then extend this length 19 times and cut. Lay the length of yarn as straight as possible in an open grassy area. Prepare a class chart similar to the one shown. Have each student estimate how many jumps it will take him to go from one end of the yarn to the other. Then direct him to test his prediction by jumping alongside the length of yarn while counting each jump. Help each child record the number of jumps on the chart where indicated. Then, as a group, compare the results. Remind students that a grasshopper travels 20 times its body length in just one jump! Who jumped the fewest number of times? Whose guess was closest to the actual number of jumps? Have fun and hop to it!

Sunny Side
(Earth Science)

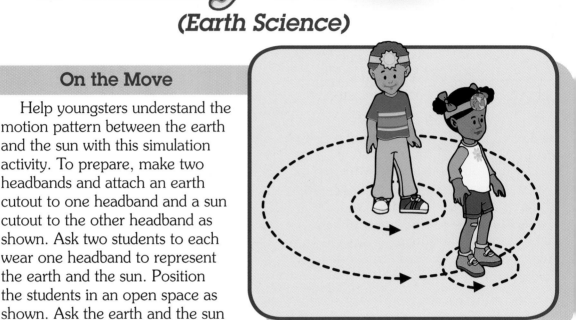

On the Move

Help youngsters understand the motion pattern between the earth and the sun with this simulation activity. To prepare, make two headbands and attach an earth cutout to one headband and a sun cutout to the other headband as shown. Ask two students to each wear one headband to represent the earth and the sun. Position the students in an open space as shown. Ask the earth and the sun to spin slowly in place. Explain that the earth and sun constantly *rotate.* Then ask the earth to continue spinning (or rotating) and slowly move around the sun. Explain that the earth rotates while it *revolves* around the sun.

Sunny Study

This investigation helps youngsters realize that the big round sun is not a solid ball, but a swirling mixture of gases. In advance, gather a clear plastic bottle, vegetable oil, and red food coloring. Half-fill the bottle with red-tinted water and then fill it to the top with vegetable oil. Secure the cap with hot glue or duct tape. Explain that the sun is made up of two gases: hydrogen and helium. Further explain that the gases are constantly in motion, which makes energy, heat, and light come off the sun. Simulate how the gases in the sun interact by shaking the bottle to mix the ingredients. Have youngsters observe the swirling motion in the bottle and compare it to the swirling gases on the sun. Then invite each child to twist and turn the bottle to investigate more.

Supersize Sun

Which is bigger: the sun or the moon? Help youngsters compare the sizes of the sun and the moon with this cooperative learning simulation. To prepare, gather two packages of M&M's candies, 40 Unifix cubes, and a roll of masking tape. Place a tape line 16 feet 8 inches long on the floor. Have students sit in a circle around the taped line. Ask youngsters if they think the sun and the moon are the same size or if one is bigger than the other. Explain that the sun's *diameter* (the straight line that passes through the center of a sphere) is much larger (about 400 times) than the moon's diameter. Show youngsters one candy and ask them to pretend it is the moon. Point to the tape line and circle of youngsters and tell them they represent the sun. Then compare the circle sun to the size of the candy moon. Ask small groups of youngsters to take turns placing candies side by side on the taped line. Have another group of children work together to count and then place a Unifix over every tenth candy. If desired, count the cubes by tens with youngsters to determine the total (400). Direct students' attention to the line of candies and tell them this is the number of moons that would fit along the diameter of the sun.

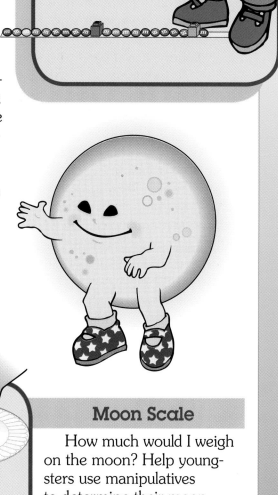

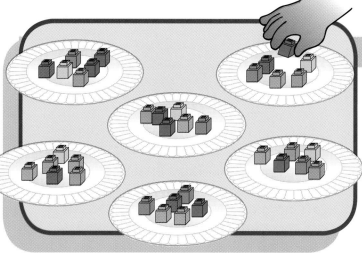

Moon Scale

How much would I weigh on the moon? Help youngsters use manipulatives to determine their moon weights with this problem-solving small-group activity. To prepare, gather a set of Unifix cubes or counting chips and six paper plates. Tell students that things on the moon weigh about one-sixth of what they weigh on earth. To demonstrate, weigh a classroom object, count out cubes to equal that number, and then divide the cubes equally onto the six plates. (For example, if a basket of blocks weighs twelve pounds, count out 12 cubes and then place two cubes on each plate. The moon weight of the blocks would be two pounds.) Now weigh each child in the group and round her weight to the nearest number that is divisible by six (36, 42, 48, etc.), and have her count out that many cubes. Help her divide the cubes onto the six plates evenly. Have her count the cubes on one plate to determine her moon weight. If desired, record each child's moon weight on a chart.

Water, Water!
(Physical Science)

Fantastic Funnels

Invite your students to pour out their prediction and inference skills as they explore water and funnels. Ahead of time, gather several plastic containers with small openings, an assortment of funnels, and some measuring cups. Put the items at your water table. Gather a small group of students and ask a volunteer to try to fill a container with water from a measuring cup (without using a funnel). What happens? Encourage youngsters to hypothesize how the container could be filled without spilling any water. Guide them to conclude that a funnel can be used to prevent water spillage. Then invite each child to use the materials to find out how fantastic funnels really are!

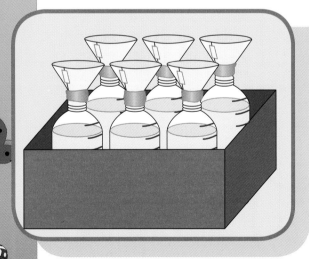

A Flood of Fun

Drench your future meteorologists with measurement skills by making these simple rain gauges. Collect a clean plastic soda bottle for each child. Have each youngster remove the label from his bottle. Then help him use a permanent marker to mark the side of his bottle in one-inch increments to make a gauge. Use a piece of overhead transparency film and duct tape to form a funnel. Then tape a funnel to the top of each gauge. Once the gauges are complete, find an unobstructed place outdoors away from trees and the school building. (Set the gauges in a plastic tub to keep them from tipping over.) After each rainfall, have your students observe their rain gauges and record the results in their science journals. You'll soon hear youngsters singing a new tune: "Rain, rain, come today. Come today to fill my rain gauge!"

Dive In!

Youngsters will dive in to this fun water experiment! In advance, fill a clear plastic two-liter bottle with water. You'll also need a plastic pen cap (without a hole in the end or plug the hole with clay as shown), a small ball of clay, and a few marbles. To make a diver, use a permanent marker to make a face on the pen cap and then press the ball of clay onto the end of it as shown. Test the weight of the diver by placing it in a cup of water. If it sinks, remove a small amount of clay and test again until it floats. Have a child drop marbles and the diver into the plastic bottle and secure the cap. Ask youngsters to observe and describe the diver and the marbles. *(The diver floats and the marbles sink.)* Have a child squeeze the the bottle as others observe the diver sinking to the bottom of the bottle. Ask youngsters to hypothesize why the diver floats and then sinks and the marbles just sink. *(An air bubble trapped inside the cap makes the diver float. When the bottle is squeezed, the water squashes the air bubble and more water goes into the cap, causing the diver to sink. The marbles are solid with no air bubbles to make them float.)*

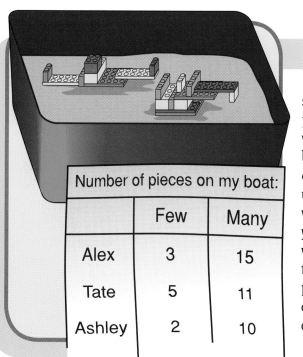

Number of pieces on my boat:		
	Few	Many
Alex	3	15
Tate	5	11
Ashley	2	10

Float My Boat!

Little boat builders will love this small-group water exploration. To prepare, fill a tub with blue-tinted water and place a set of plastic building blocks beside it. Invite a small group of youngsters to explore and build until they have made something that will float in the water. Challenge youngsters to create a floating boat with *as few* pieces as possible and then build another one with *as many* pieces as possible. Have each group count and record their findings on a chart as shown.

Ooh, Ocean!

(Earth Science)

Build a Beach

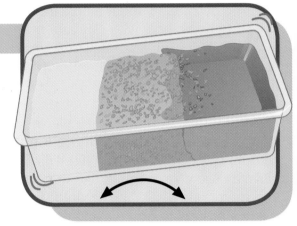

If a field trip to the beach is out of the question, bring the beach into the classroom with this sandy demonstration. Fill the left third of a clear plastic tub with an inch or so of sand. Then put the same amount of aquarium gravel in the middle portion of the tub. Finally, pour $1\frac{1}{2}$ to two cups of water into the right side of the tub. Now encourage youngsters to watch as you hold the tub and tilt it gently from left to right, making waves. As waves form, they'll wash through the rocks and sand and distribute the material pretty evenly over the entire tub. Explain to your students that water wears down rock, helps form sand, and carries sand to form beaches. Just beachy!

Ocean Motion

Gentle ocean waves will pull youngsters to this relaxing simulation activity. To prepare, half-fill a clean 20-ounce plastic bottle with blue-tinted water. Then add clear vegetable oil to fill the bottle. Add a few plastic toys (such as fish and a boat) and a few small seashells to the bottle and replace the cap (if desired, secure the cap with hot glue). Ask youngsters to observe the ocean motion as you gently rock the bottle back and forth as shown. Have children take turns making waves with the bottle. Encourage them to observe the action of the toys and shells within the waves. If desired, have each child illustrate her observations on paper and then combine all the illustrations into a class booklet.

Lots of Light

(Physical Science)

Reflections

Shine light on the science of reflections with this simple demonstration. You will need a file folder, a piece of foil, a white piece of construction paper, a black piece of construction paper, tape, a flashlight, scissors, and a yellow sun cutout. Cut out the center of the sun and tape the remaining frame to the end of the flashlight as shown. Now tape the edges of the foil to the left side of the folder. Stand the folder on end. Shine the flashlight at the foil. Adjust the right side of the folder so that it catches the reflected light. Point out to your students the brightness and strength of this reflection. Now replace the foil with white paper. Ask students whether they think the reflection will be brighter than the foil. Have a student volunteer check the predictions. Continue in this same manner with the black paper. What conclusions can your little ones make about colors and reflections? *(Surfaces differ in how much light they reflect. White surfaces and metallic surfaces reflect light well and dark surfaces reflect little light.)*

Spoon Spoofs

Your students will scoop up spoonfuls of learning in this small-group investigation. Give each child in a group a small pocket mirror and a metal spoon. Have her examine both items and name the similarities and differences. Direct the child to look into the mirror and study her reflection for a few seconds. Then instruct her to find her reflection on the back of the spoon. Is there a difference? Ask the child to predict how her reflection will look in the bowl of the spoon. Have the child flip the spoon over and look into the bowl of the spoon. Her reflection is upside down! Why? The surface of the bowl of the spoon is indented, or *concave,* and reflects light away from the center which flips the image. How illuminating!

Moving Motion

(Physical Science)

Get Moving!

Take the opportunity to introduce science concepts about motion as youngsters play on the playground. Gather a small group of students around a swing. Invite a volunteer to sit still in the swing. Ask children whether the swing is moving. Then have children explain why it is not moving and what must be done to get it moving. Direct the child in the swing to start swinging. Have the others observe and explain what he is doing with his body to make the swing move. Lead students to conclude that the volunteer makes the swing move by *pushing* and *pulling* his body. To extend the learning, have students brainstorm other things that have to be pushed or pulled into motion, such as a door and a wagon.

Pushes and Pulls

Push it, pull it—youngsters will have so much fun playing with toys that they won't realize they are learning a science concept! To prepare, collect a variety of toys that need to be either pushed or pulled to move. Then take your students and the collection of objects outdoors. Encourage each child to take a turn with a toy and make it move. Then have each child report whether he had to push or pull the toy. Make a simple graph similar to the one shown to help each child record his results. Then have him read the graph to determine whether he had more pushes or pulls.

Socks, Shoes, and More

Make pushes and pulls a little more personal as youngsters practice fine-motor skills. To prepare, stock the dramatic-play center with dolls and a variety of doll clothes. Then ask youngsters to think about how they dressed to come to school. Have them name the clothing or accessories that needed to be pushed or pulled to get dressed. For example, socks need to be pulled on and buttons need to be pushed through the buttonholes. Invite a small group of youngsters to visit the center and demonstrate pushes and pulls as they change the dolls' clothing.

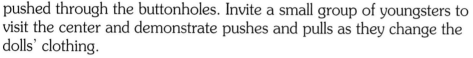

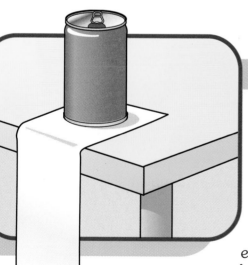

Stay Still

After summertime thirsts are quenched, save the empty cans for this moving experiment. To prepare, cut a class supply of 3" x 11" strips of copy paper. Demonstrate the following activity for youngsters and then invite small groups to repeat the activity. Place about one-third of a strip on a table's edge and then put the empty can on top of it—leaving two-thirds of the strip hanging down. Tell youngsters that you want to pull the strip out from under the can *without* moving the can. Encourage students to brainstorm different ways that this activity may be done. Then hold the dangling end of the strip straight out with one hand and quickly karate-chop the middle of the strip with the other hand. The can should still be on the table, but the paper strip won't be. *(The paper strip is lighter than the can; therefore, it can be moved more quickly and with less force than the can.)*

Rock On

(Earth Science)

Timely Tools

Give your students a lesson in how rocks were used as tools many years ago with this small-group activity. In advance, collect several plastic children's garden tools and a hand-sized rock for each child in a small group. Take youngsters outside and have each child use a rock to try to dig a hole in the ground. Then have each child use a tool to dig. Ask children to compare the differences between the two tools and how easy or difficult digging was with each one. Guide them to understand that the tool's shape and handle make using it much easier than using the rock. Ask youngsters to brainstorm ways the rock could be used as a tool.

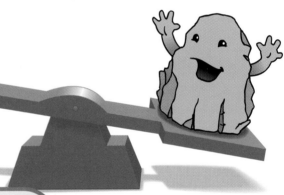

Let's Rock

Youngsters will turn over every rock to complete this measurement exploration. To prepare, collect a balance scale and rocks of different sizes and shapes. Also, collect several different classroom objects to use on the balance scale. Then ask a small group of children to explore the rocks and try to find two rocks that balance the scale. For more problem solving, ask them to determine whether a flat rock is heavier than a round rock, or to find a small rock that is heavier than a big rock. Then give students the objects collected and have them balance each one with rocks. Encourage the group to count how many rocks it takes to balance each object. Rock on!

Space Place
(Earth Science)

One Small Step

No air, wind, or water—help youngsters realize the moon is different from Earth as they step into this experiment. In advance, gather two shoeboxes filled with moist sand. Tell youngsters that the moon has no air or weather as Earth does. Then have a child make a footprint in each sandbox. Place one box on a shelf where it won't be disturbed to represent conditions on the moon. Place the other box outside in the weather to represent conditions on Earth. Have children observe each sandbox later to see whether there are any changes. Compare the two footprints after several days and discuss the differences.

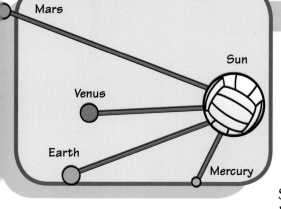

So Much Space

Help future astronauts understand the Earth in relation to the sun with this comparison activity. To prepare, collect a volleyball, four pieces of string (lengths: one yard, two yards, 2½ yards, four yards), and four different-sized beads. Tie each bead onto one piece of string. Read *Me and My Place in Space* by Joan Sweeney to acquaint youngsters with the solar system and outer space. Refer to a solar system illustration or draw one on chart paper to point out the location of Earth in relation to the sun. Place the volleyball on the floor and ask youngsters to pretend it is the sun. Then place the four stringed beads out from the sun to represent Mercury, Venus, Earth, and Mars as shown. Compare the size relationship of the planets to the sun. Explain to youngsters that the remaining four planets (Jupiter, Saturn, Uranus, and Neptune) are so far from the sun that on the model they would be outside the classroom!

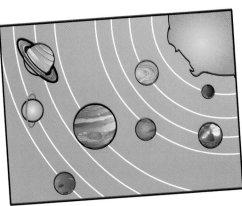

Energetic Exercise

(Life Science)

Stretching Sprouts

Little sprouts will learn about the life cycle of a flower as they stretch through this flexibility activity. Ask youngsters to pretend they are seeds snuggled underground by curling up on the floor. Have one child pretend to water the seeds and have another child pretend to make a sun (with arms forming a circle overhead) over the little seeds. Then have the seeds slowly stretch to grow upward until they are standing straight up. Add more water and sunshine. Encourage little ones to stretch, stretch, stretch arms out to bloom into beautiful flowers. Finally, have one child pretend to blow cold weather over the little flowers until they wilt onto the ground as they carefully sit down. Explain to youngsters that daily stretching exercises can be fun and will help keep their muscles healthy and flexible.

Flap and Fly

Youngsters will get a quick burst of energy as they learn how movement raises their heartbeat. Ask each child to pretend he is a baby bird getting ready for his first flying lesson. First, help him feel his heartbeat by placing two fingers on his neck. Then have him begin to flap his wings and slowly increase the action. Encourage him to pretend to fly through the air. Then have all the little birds come in for a landing by circling their arms slowly and squatting as shown. Help each child check his heartbeat again. Encourage children to compare the change in heartbeat before and after the activity. Explain to them that the heart pumps blood throughout the body and exercise helps strengthen the heart.